WHICH CAME FIRST?

ISBN 979-8-89112-152-2 (Paperback)
ISBN 979-8-89112-641-1 (Hardcover)
ISBN 979-8-89112-153-9 (Digital)

Covenant Books
11661 Hwy 707
Murrells Inlet, SC 29576
www.covenantbooks.com

WHICH CAME FIRST?

Margaret Klump

Illustrated by Marcia Crots

CHAPTER 1

You have heard the question, "Which came first? The chicken or the egg?" Since schoolchildren are taught that everything we see came into existence, over millions of years, by evolutionary process, I decided to take a crack at figuring out just *how* it all could have happened!

So here goes! Let's take a look at the egg being the first thing formed since it is small and much less complex than a chicken, which has a head, beak, heart, lungs, and legs!

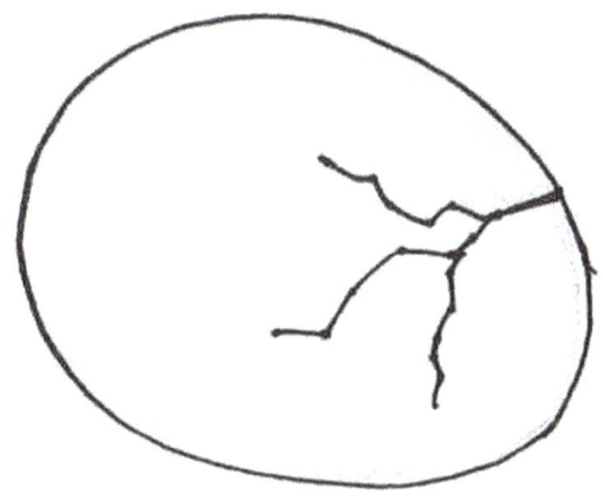

The egg is a simple little object, with a yolk and a white inside. From what I understand, the baby chick is formed out of the white of the egg, with the yolk being its means of nourishment during the time it takes to go from an egg to a chicken inside the shell!

If you want to read something really interesting, look up how a baby chick is formed inside the eggshell—very complicated, actually, but after twenty-one days of being kept warm by the mother hen, out pops a fully-formed chick that knows how to scratch with its claws and begin feeding itself after it dries off and begins to move around on tiny legs!

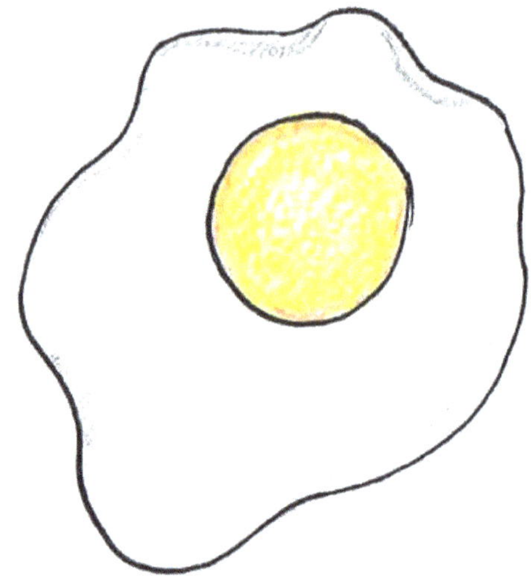

Wait a minute! If evolution brought all this about, how can the egg turn into a baby chick in just twenty-one days? That's not even a month, let alone one hundred years, or even a thousand years!

But let's stick to the cold, hard facts here! Baby chicks develop in twenty-one *days*!

Okay, the baby pecks its way out of the shell. That action gives the baby some strength, and when it staggers out, it is wet—not too cute—but dries off quickly into a fluffy baby chick!

Now it needs to have some food and water. Hopefully, there is something in the evolutionary mud to supply the needs of the baby, and it grows into adulthood. Google says this takes eighteen weeks, which translates into about five months. Now that baby is getting ready to lay eggs itself! Progress! It didn't take a million years, a thousand years, or a hundred years—-not *one* year but *five months*!

But wait! In order for the eggs Mrs. Hen lays to hatch into more baby chicks, she needs a little help from Mr. Rooster! "It takes two to tango." I'm sure you have heard that expression, and unless *another* egg formed in the primeval mud with a male chick inside, at the very same time the female chick formed, and trusting that neither of them falls prey to a developing cat or dog, this is the end of the road for the propagation of the species! Somehow the "millions of years" theory doesn't work at *all* on eggs!

So let's forget about the egg coming first. Let's check out the "chicken first" part of the old question!

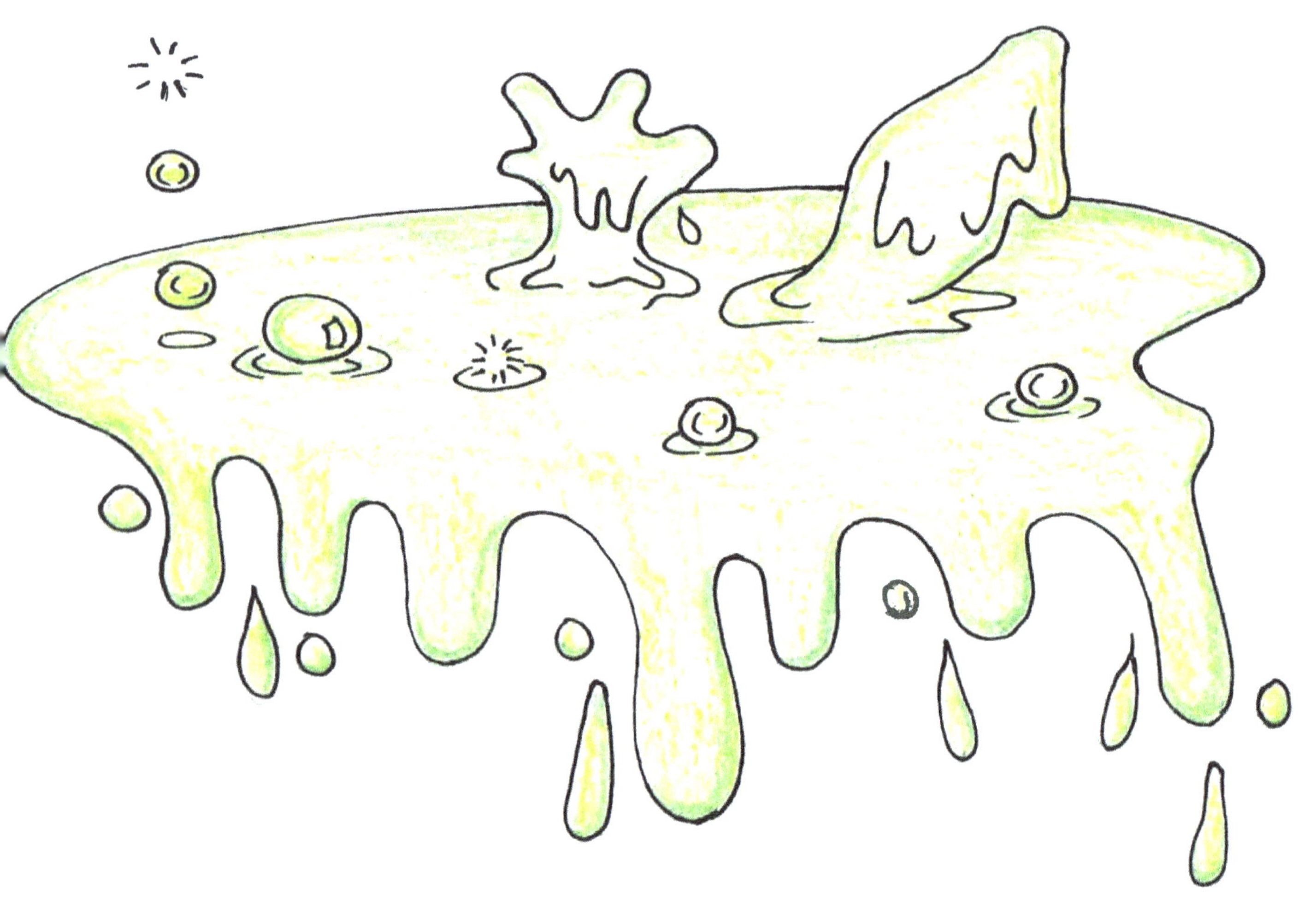

CHAPTER 2

Let's watch as a chicken is formed in the ooze of primeval evolution! Which part is going to form first? The heart, the lungs, the digestive system, or a body of some sort? Seems as though the body would have to come first in order to hold the insides together! That just makes sense, right?

So here comes the beginning of a chicken body out of the slime. What does it look like? It would have to have some basic meat on it, or it couldn't evolve into a whole, feathered chicken! So the evolutionary process begins with perhaps a wing. Soon, a second wing is formed on the other side of the emerging body, but what keeps this hunk of flesh from disintegrating? You take any piece of meat and put it out in the elements, and it rots and gets stinky real fast!

The only natural thing to keep it from going bad would be if the weather was freezing! But we all know nothing moves in a frozen state, and nothing grows outside in wintertime so that idea isn't going to work! So this beginning chicken *has* to have some life in it somehow! Does it have a beginning heart? But a piece of a heart would not work, unless it had all four chambers, and add to that, the heart needs to beat to move blood around inside the tissue to keep it alive! Hmm, we have run into a roadblock of sorts here!

How is this hunk of beginning chicken going to keep from rotting away, unless it has some means of keeping it alive, and that means blood flow? Any living animal, like a chicken, needs blood to keep it alive. That goes for us humans too! In earlier centuries, doctors ignorantly bled sick patients, hopefully, to make the patient better. Of course, it killed the poor victim.

These days, blood transfusions save many lives because the life of the flesh is *in* the *blood*! Okay, suppose the heart has developed, and there are blood vessels running through the chunk of flesh, but blood needs oxygenation, does it not? Now we suddenly have to have some lungs and a mouth to breathe in air!

Does this chunk of chicken have a mouth, which means having a head with an opening with a throat to get the air to the lungs to help the heart keep alive? Somehow this does not fit with millions and millions of years of development!

In fact, the more millions of years you add, the more improbable—*impossible* this whole scenario becomes!

Chicken's Respiratory System

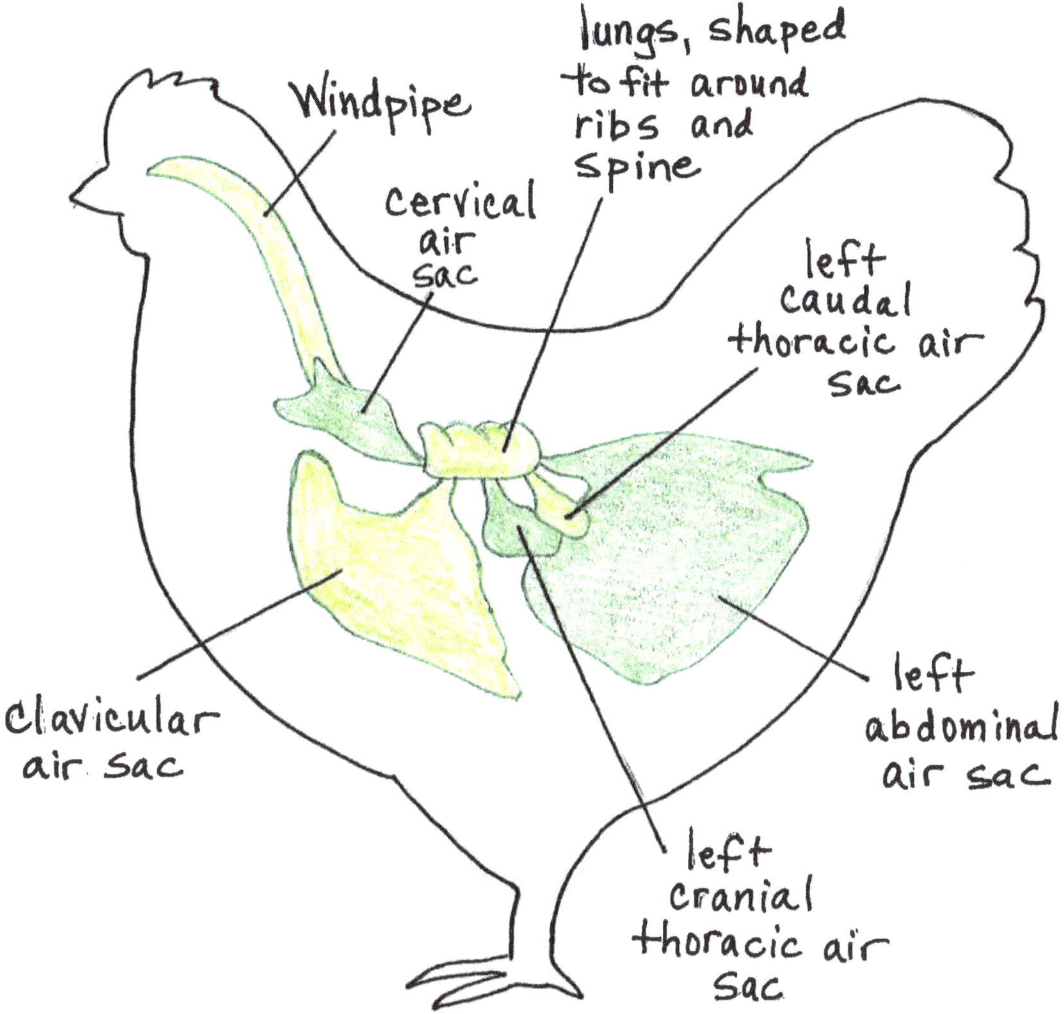

So in order for this chicken body to maintain itself, it has to have life. And to have life, it has to have a method to breathe. So lungs are an immediate necessity! But how can it breathe unless it has fully developed lungs, plus a nose or mouth? This means this chicken body needs a neck and a head with a beak! Could this have all taken place all *at once* in the act of creation—oops! I mean, *evolution*? It *had* to if this poor emerging creature was going to survive.

So we have a body, formed out of the ooze, with a working set of lungs *and* a head, with a beak on it, plus a working heart and a circulatory system. In order for this whole apparatus to continue living, it needs sustenance. So not only does this chicken body have to have a blood flow with a heart and a set of lungs with a head for breathing, but it also has to have a digestive system and a need for a mouth and throat to sustain life!

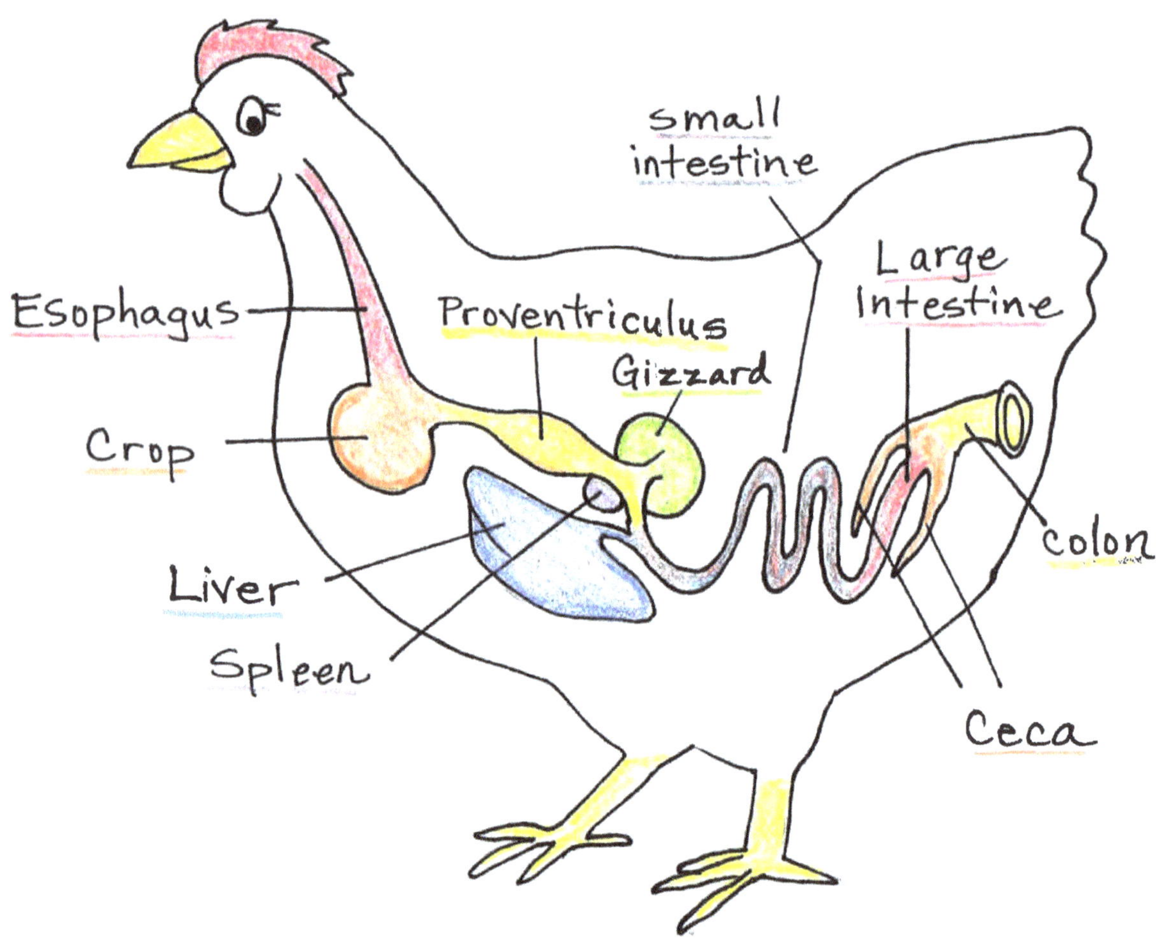

The more you think about it, the more things need to be in place before this chicken can begin to put on feathers and start the process of *life*!

If it needs food, it needs two fully developed eyes to find the food *and* feet to get it around for the food sources!

How this *all* can take place on its own is simply unreal! The more millions of years you add to the story, the more improbable it becomes! Chickens live five to ten years, according to Google. They had to be able to replace themselves very quickly or the species would have gone extinct before they even got started. There has to be a male *and* a female, or you get nowhere very fast!

This evolutionary process is vastly, totally *impossible* when you take a look at how it might have happened. This is checking out how a simple chicken could have evolved! What about cows, horses, pigs, and alligators?

Their evolution would have been even more complex. Then think about *you*! Your body is a marvel of design, and wherever there is design, there is a designer doing the work behind the scenes.

So we see that the proposed evolutionary process simply is a figment of imagination, and the millions of years proposed to be the answer to how it all occurred is a humungous, ridiculous explanation of our origins by those who push it. So just *how* did our chicken come into existence? We know it did—we have chicken on our plates regularly, and we all enjoy cakes made with chicken eggs! There is only *one* explanation, which the evolutionists refuse to recognize, *God* made the chicken!

CHAPTER 3

Yes, indeed, God *did* make the chicken first. It says so, in Genesis, the first book of the Bible! You can read it for yourself. The twenty-fourth verse reads, "Then God said, 'Let the earth bring forth living creatures (chickens, ducks, crows, rabbits, and dogs) after their kind; cattle and creeping things and beasts of the earth (lions, tigers, and elephants) after their kind' and it was so." The animals were created by God in *one* day!

It *has* to be *God*. He made the hummingbird that feeds while its wings whir at an astounding sixty beats per second; the buzzard that can locate dead carrion on which it feeds, the robin that builds its nest and feeds its young on bugs and worms, the swallow that tends her young by carrying away their waste from the nest until they get big enough to do their business over the edge of the nest—imagine what the nest would be like if those four hungry babies pooped inside the nest! They would be unable to live in such squalor, so God designed Mom and Dad to carry it all away for a time!

Notice that he made creatures "after their kind." You don't see a fowl that is half turkey, half goose. There are no mixtures of robins and crows. They procreate "after their kind." In fact, when people breed a horse and a donkey, the resultant mule is not able to reproduce itself. It is sterile!

And last of all, God created Adam and Eve, who began to procreate until today when we have almost eight billion people walking on God's green earth, enjoying *all* he has provided—air, water, food, and gravity—which keeps us from flying off the face of the earth. He knew *exactly* what we needed, and he provided it with his loving hands.

Look around you at the marvels he has created! Your eyes are wonderful examples of his handiwork; you have two of them, which gives you depth perception. They focus instantly on things close by or far away, they see vibrant colors, and they keep themselves clean with a watering system that also serves as a lubricant so they don't dry up.

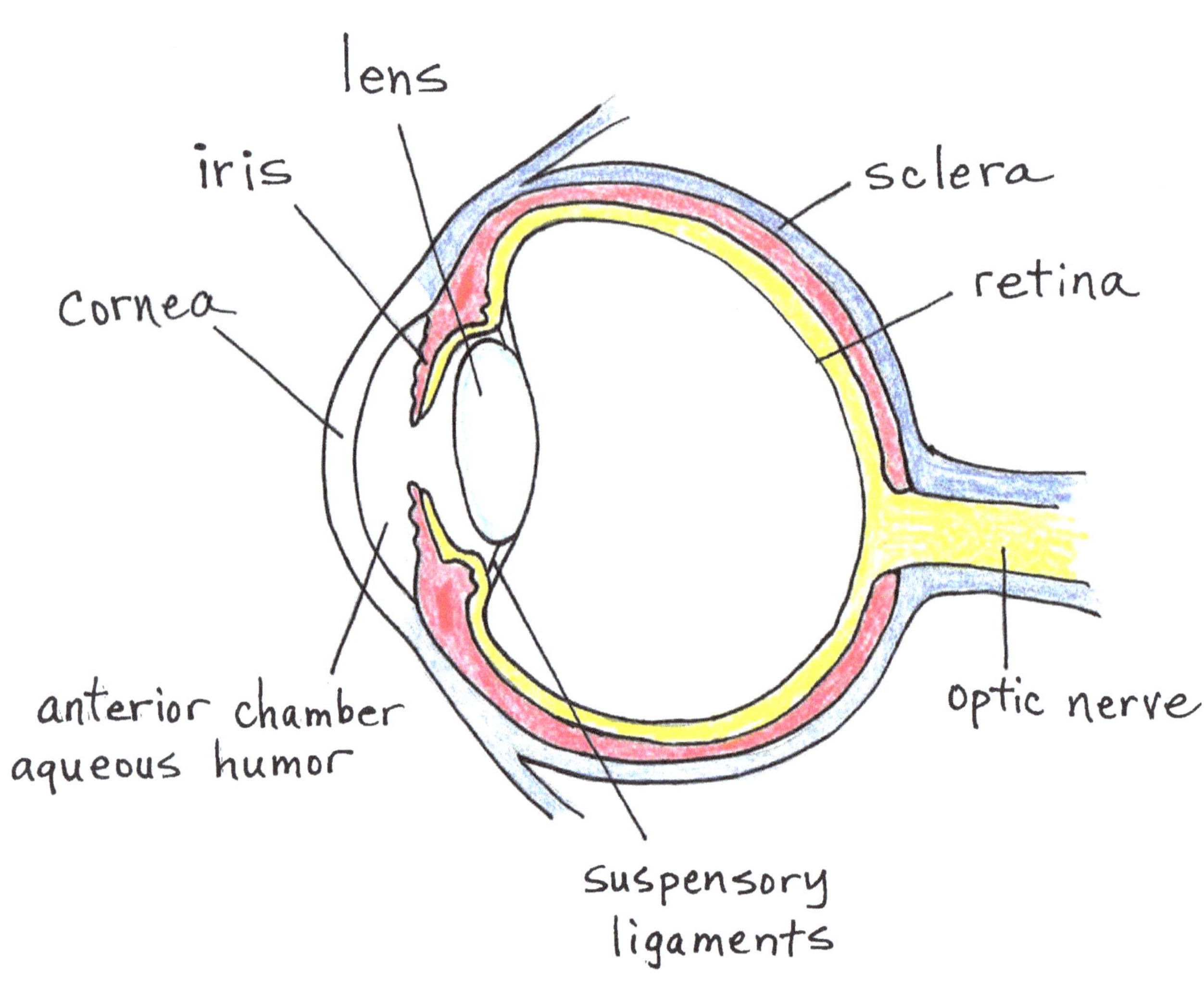

Yes, the God who made you and me has provided us with a means of sheltering our bodies, keeping them well-fed (sometimes *too* much so). We have legs to carry us wherever we choose, hands that are marvels of engineering, with opposing thumbs that give us the ability to grasp things.

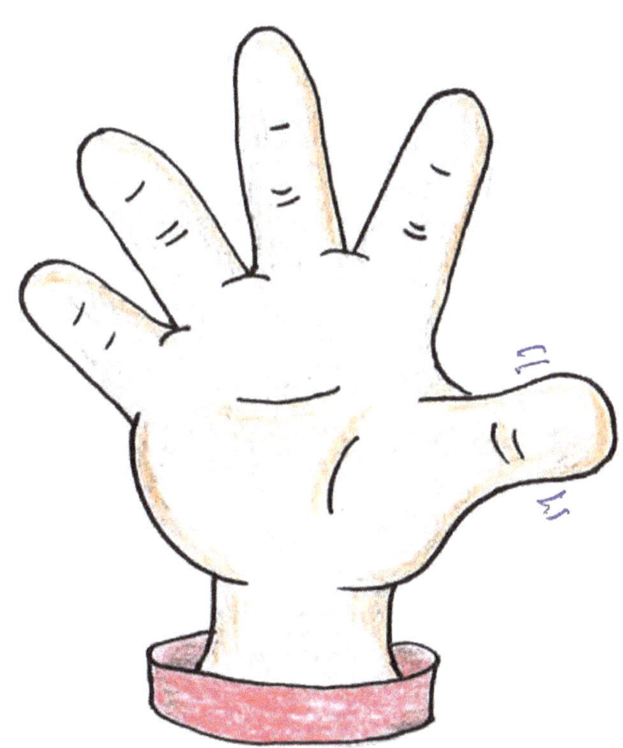

However, people have a way of wanting to do what they like, and all of us are born with a sinful nature. Parents have to *teach* their kids to tell the truth and not take what belongs to someone else! Our first parents, Adam and Eve, chose to do their own thing and ate from a tree that they had been told to leave alone by God. Their self-will is passed on to all their progeny—you and me included!

He paid with his life for your sin of lying, stealing, and cursing by dying on the cross of Calvary nearly two thousand years ago, and when we truly believe that he did that for *me* and confess to him our need and our repentance for our sinful ways, he comes into our life and forgives our sins.

When you take your last breath on this earth, you will take the next breath in the very heaven He is preparing for those who love him and trust in his forgiveness!

Yes, indeed. The chicken came first by the very hand of an almighty, loving *God*!

I want to acknowledge my daughter, Marcia Crots
and her fine illustrations for this book.

ABOUT THE AUTHOR

I have lived in Michigan most of my life. My first eight years of learning were spent in a two-room school with no running water; an outhouse was behind the school, and we drank water from a bucket that was filled each morning from a pump in the schoolyard. I married a farm boy, and we spent sixty-two years farming together. We reared seven children and today have eighteen grandchildren and twenty-two great-grands. I have great concern for today's children, rudderless in an increasingly godless world.

www.ingramcontent.com/pod-product-compliance
Lightning Source LLC
Chambersburg PA
CBHW040157110726
48005CB00018B/2801